D1087251

JUDAH
WHO ALWAYS SAID
"NO!"

Written by Harriet K. Feder
Illustrated by Katherine Janus Kahn

KAR-BEN COPIES, INC.   ROCKVILLE, MD

To my grandchildren, Ben, Ari and Michael
—H.K.F.

Feder, Harriet K.
   Judah who always said, "No!" / Harriet K. Feder; illustrated by Katherine Janus Kahn.
   p.   cm.
   Summary: Brave Judah, a leader in the resistance to the changes a Greek king tries to force upon the Jews of Jerusalem, takes part in a stunning victory celebrated today as Hanukkah.
   ISBN 0-929371-13-5 : — ISBN 0-929371-14-3 (pbk.) :
   1. Judas, Maccabeus, d. 161 B.C.—Juvenile literature. 2. Jews—Kings and rulers—Biography—Juvenile literature. 3. Hanukkah—Juvenile literature. [1. Jews—History—586 B.C.-70 A.D. 2. Judas, Maccabeus, d. 161 B.C. 3. Hannukah.] I. Kahn, Katherine, ill. II. Title.
DS121.8.J8F43   1990
933'.04'092—dc20
[B]   90-4854
                                                                 CIP

Text copyright © 1990 by Harriet K. Feder
Illustrations copyright © 1990 by Katherine Janus Kahn
All rights reserved. No portion of this book may be reproduced without the written permission of the publisher.
Published by KAR-BEN COPIES, INC. Rockville, MD   1-800-4-KARBEN
Printed in the United States of America

The Story of Hanukkah

More than 2,000 years ago, a Syrian king, Antiochus IV, ruled over Israel. He tried to force the Jews to follow Greek traditions. Many refused. A small band of Jews, under the leadership of Judah Maccabee, fought the mighty armies of Antiochus and won. When they returned to restore their Holy Temple in Jerusalem, they found only enough oil to keep the Temple menorah burning for one day. But a miracle happened, and the oil burned for eight days. Today, Jews all over the world celebrate Hanukkah to recall the Maccabees' victory.

Long ago in Jerusalem there lived a boy named Judah, who was always saying, "NO!"

"Ready for your nap, Judah?" his mother asked when he was very small.

"NO!" said Judah. "I'm playing with my toy sword."

"Come, I will tell you a story about three bears," said his father.

"NO!" said Judah. "I want a story about three soldiers."

"We're going out to play," called Judah's brothers. "Follow us."

"NO!" said Judah. "I don't want to follow. I want to lead."

When Judah grew up, a wicked Greek king ruled over Jerusalem. "All the Jews under my rule must change their names to Greek names," the king's messenger commanded.

"NO!" said Judah.
"I will not change my
name. I like my Hebrew
name."

"All the Jews under my rule must stop studying and work out in the gym instead," the king commanded.

"NO!" said Judah. "My muscles are big enough. I must continue to study and learn how to think."

"All the Jews under my rule must pray to my gods," roared
the king. "And they must bow down to my idols."

"**NO!**" said Judah. "You have too many gods. You have a god for the sun, a god for the moon, a god for almost everything. The Jews pray to only One God."

The king was angry that the Jews would not pray to his gods.
He ordered his soldiers to destroy the Temple in Jerusalem.

They stole the gold and silver
and put one of the king's idols
on the altar.

"The king has destroyed our Temple," the Jews cried.
"He will destroy us next."

"NO!" said Judah, "We will not let him destroy us.
We will escape to the mountains and hide."

"The king's soldiers are many and strong," the people said.
"Their muscles will help them win."

"NO!" said Judah. "We have studied long and hard.
We know how to think."

Everyone thought and thought. They scratched their heads. They rubbed their beards. The sun went down. The moon came up. Still they kept on thinking. Soon the sun was up again.

"Let's fight the soldiers right now," someone said.

"NO!" said Judah. "We must wait until dark and surprise them."

So the Jews waited and waited until the daylight was gone. Then Judah put on his great shield and took his spear in his hand.

"Follow me," he called. And he led them into battle.

"Judah strikes like a hammer," the king's soldiers cried, and they ran from the Jewish fighters.

When the battle was over, the brave Jews wanted to rest.

"NO!" said Judah. "Now we must rebuild the Temple and give thanks to God."

Judah led the Jews back to Jerusalem. They dragged the king's idol from the Temple and smashed it into bits. They hammered and sawed and scrubbed and rubbed until the Temple was holy once more.

"We've found only one jar of pure oil," someone cried. "It is barely enough for one day. We cannot light the menorah."

"NO!" said Judah. "We must light the lamp. Surely God will help us."

So the Jews lit the menorah. And a miracle happened. The little jar of oil burned for eight whole days.

"Let us celebrate this great miracle," the people shouted.

And this time, Judah said,

"YES!"